HOMAGE TO LONGSHOT O'LEARY

POEMS

REGINALD GIBBONS

OTHER BOOKS BY REGINALD GIBBONS

POETRY

Roofs Voices Roads
The Ruined Motel
Saints
Maybe It Was So
Sparrow: New and Selected Poems

FICTION

Five Pears or Peaches
Sweetbitter

TRANSLATION

Selected Poems of Luis Cernuda
Guillén on Guillén: The Poetry and the Poet (edited and translated with A. L. Geist)

CRITICISM

William Goyen: A Study of the Short Fiction

EDITED VOLUMES

The Poet's Work
New Writing from Mexico
Criticism in the University (edited with Gerald Graff)
The Writer in Our World
Thomas McGrath: Life and the Poem (edited with Terrence des Pres)

EDITIONS

William Goyen, *Had I a Hundred Mouths*
William Goyen, *Half a Look of Cain*

HOMAGE TO LONGSHOT O'LEARY

POEMS *for Maureen*
with every good hope
for you & your work
Reg

REGINALD GIBBONS

HOLY COW! PRESS • DULUTH, MINNESOTA • 1999

The author thanks the editors of the following journals and anthologies, in which some of these
poems first appeared, in one version or another: *Chicago Review, Common Knowledge, Connecticut
Review, Crazy Horse, Great River Review, Many Mountains Moving, Ontario Review, Paris Review,
Poetry East, Quarterly Review of Literature, Salmagundi, Tendril, Third Coast.*

The author also thanks the Alice Berline Kaplan Center for the Humanities at Northwestern
University for leave time when some of these poems were completed.

"Poetry After the Recent War" was first published in *After the Storm*, ed. by Jay Meek and F. D.
Reeve, Washington D.C.: Maisonneuve Press, 1992.

Library of Congress Cataloging-in-Publication Data

Gibbons, Reginald.
    Homage to Longshot O'Leary : poems / Reginald Gibbons.
        p.   cm.
    ISBN 0-930100-85-9
    1. McGrath, Thomas, 1916-   —Poetry   I. Title.
  PS3557.I1392H65   1999
  811 ' .54—dc21   98-42755
                                    CIP

Holy Cow! Press titles are distributed to the trade by Consortium Book Sales & Distribution,
1045 Westgate Drive, Saint Paul, Minnesota 55114. Our books are available through all major
library distributors and jobbers, and through most small press distributors, including
Bookpeople and Small Press Distribution. For personal orders and other inquiries, write to:

Holy Cow! Press
Post Office Box 3170
Mount Royal Station
Duluth, Minnesota 55803

In memory of T.M. and T.D.P.

Together

Rain through the spring night.
Pulse of waters beating on the pavement.
Song of water splashing from
that high broken gutter that needs
fixing.
          New small rivers for tonight.
Down them, even up them, some
hope always moves, some movement
always carries hope.
           Through the spring night, rain.

Contents

1

A Meeting

While the unaware world is both opening and closing toward our future
on this night of sparkling gusts and frozen pavements,
inside a shabby little upstairs auditorium
thirty or so are gathered to honor the undaunted
long-lived hero
(while she thinks of her secret despair from time to time, of retreats she did not let others see, of
        rising again and again in the teeth of cold winds, of the campaign that is about to begin),
to praise her resolve and stamina
(which she has maintained thanks to her mother's love or her father's, when she was young;
or despite their indifference, but because of the love, when she was young, of some teacher or
        aunt who opened a way for her, and whom she cannot thank now because the years have
        closed behind her),

and we all sit together on folding chairs arranged (by a faithful keeper of our hope, who came
        early) in careful rows on the cracked, scuffed, peeling linoleum floor,
we listen to tributes both flowery and plain, both fluent and stammering
(from the simple person who looks anxiously at the hero while speaking
and from the confident experienced operative who, having lived far more than could be told, tells
        some of what remains to be lived),

and in the first row of chairs the hero bows her gray-haired head,
and the hour is passing,
and, because the old window which someone opened in order to let out the accumulated heat now
        lets too much cold from the brute night into the shabby little upstairs auditorium, a
        woman from the back row of the folding chairs now disarranged on the cracked, scuffed,
        peeling linoleum floor goes to that window and as quietly as she can, while another
        tribute is being offered, she draws it downward and closed
(although one pane is already broken out anyway
as if the hero herself, stronger than the rest of us, insisting
on our behalf, had arrived secretly before any of us and deliberately shattered it).

Outtake from a Monologue in Progress

While Dads are saying, "Son, go cut a switch,"
Moms work out their daughters' Mix 'n' Match.

It's a game that anyone can play—
punish; then indulge and make it seem a plea.

"I didn't mean to be so negative,"
I'll say, but who can show me what to save?

Wonder won't come clear, and what good's faith
when you work and tube yourself to death?

I gave up asking where to find a hero—
not me nor you, not grunts, not Capt. Zero.

Cause all these ramdamnbunctious boys are just
as mean as they look—they're not the ones I'd trust.

Who do they work for is what I'd want to know.
And what should I be working for, and who.

There's forty wars at once, and TV ads!
People put down the jews, latinos, bloods.

Something's needed, that much I can see,
against it all, something bigger than me.

I know that innocence and tears won't work.
It's not a time for that, good hearts seem dark.

Not dark, maybe—though light is hard to find.
It isn't easy, bringing good to mind.

Is it sheer crowd size, squeezing us till we break?
What looks like single acts is a group mistake.

They say that it's our own fault things are bad.
If we didn't do this to ourselves, who did?

There's lots of power in the hands of them that own—
But nearly none in a person fighting alone.

We need some air, some work to do, some call
that wasn't thought up by a dollar bill.

What's work? Nightmares, a struggle to survive
the boss and kids, to sell, to medevac alive?

We need instructions, privacy and hope,
a way to be, with others. Not candy and dope.

For there's a barking in the night, far off, unblessed.
Do those who once were holy come back merciless?

Affidavit from the Future

I came out of what was not my mother.
When my eyes cracked open in the light
and I looked up, I saw a germ-lamp,
a bulb that disinfected as it shone.

Over me rode my father's head commanding—
I later learned—a body that was not his.
He never told me where he got it,
only that it had been left-handed, before.

In school I was trained to work
twenty years, and to like that work, and then
to come to dislike it and quit. They have
solved the problem of unemployment in this way.

At last my mother decided it was enough.
She ratified (that's the term
we use) her wish by refusing the treatment
and the alternative. For that too she was trained.

A desert is growing inside us, she said at the end.
And it's true that red rock is our principal icon:
blood, rust, the mythical rose—those color
our meditation in the aluminum shrine.

Yet we continue to eat and sleep; we drink
a variety of wines. To discover wherein
the germ of our culture lies preserved
is the great task of our researchers.

They have solved the problem of the life
of the mind, for although the artificial wood
is rationed, we may use it at times, and not knowing whence
the ancient flame leapt up, we are kept occupied with wonder.

I came out of what was not my mother
and when I first drew breath
it was in the room where the cow had been.
Its womb, its blood, its milk were mine

but the last stage was not to my liking,
the taste of burnt flesh on the point of my knife.

BOY ON A BUSY CORNER

Arriving from some station with his one bag,
an alligator-plastic cardboard suitcase

of a sort to raise pity
when I look back at him after walking by,

here he has come, we all know, uncounted times over the decades,
speaking to himself silently, trying not to turn his head so violently

to follow what he sees, and walking marked by awe
on the streets of the city strugglers, so visibly

unlike them yet already becoming at least a little
like them, not in success (even if only the success of

simply living in the city) but in the burdens of knowing
their disappointments, their sustained unrealized plans,

their stance and gait of anxiousness or hurry or
determined nonchalance, the city

style, the shoes and coats and clasping of the hands
of their children for whom enough could not be provided,

from whom disappointment could not long be held off
outside the great store windows, far below the old

office ledges, the new glass parapets, and what he does not yet know of:
the copied documents and bills of lading, the gleaming tray

of cool dry crystal tumblers ready for champagne in the boardroom,
the tired, uninvited reps elevatoring down thirty or fifty floors

to make at least one more call, the pharaonic lobby
with presiding guard and metonymical directory.

Everything he sees and hears is a first wonder
in the midst of the only half-crowded streets, especially

the guitar-playing blues singer whose mojo is always working,
her howling mutt right with her, and that unforgettable scar on her forehead.

Some knowledge returned to me that I had stood here,
that I was here before I ever arrived, or he, and then did arrive.

That I came as, I came in, every earlier incarnation of every desire
to arrive, to have come to a center of things,

where possibilities could not be counted on
the fingers of even two hands if they really were possible.

Here he was, leaning out, looking up the wide noisy streets
that lie deep between big stone, big steel, buildings, a boy,

a young man, on his own, not yet knowing those things that I need
to know, perhaps able to stop dreaming, to understand,

to assess fully, to hope yet to hold back his invisible horse,
to find for himself some work, some friend, some beautiful girl.

In a Bar with CNN on TV

One guy in particular kind of sums everything up.
He's a grinning salesman who rushes in with his sample case of arms and torment and when I
        won't shake his hand (See? No weapon.) he goes undaunted past two women to the next man.

They shake hands.
Talking with that guy, he makes the sale.
Their grinning is a shrieking noise like metal being sawn; it gets louder and louder.

He catches a fly in his hand without killing it
and then stuns it by throwing it against the wall.
He picks it up, ties one end of the finest of threads around it
and ties the other end to the wrist of a small standing female doll he has taken out of his sample case.

Then he picks up the doll and undresses it, without losing the fly, which is pulling at the end of its
        tether in thwarted flight.
While he covers the back of the doll with kisses
the fly lands on his face, on his ear, leaping off again each time.
Then he smashes the doll and sweeps away the fragments and the dead fly, and orders a drink.

It's now past curfew, but no one leaves.
Everybody thinks they're responsible for their own fate, and we all feel courageous.
More rounds.

Mortar fire hits the bar, we're all wounded but none of us realizes it.
Patrols come down the street, but they can see that all of us are dead and they don't bother us.

Seventy-one different brands of imported beer, two camps alternating country-western and hiphop
        on the juke, Belfast and Sarajevo on the TV.

I watch myself.
There's a kind of life in this hopelessness.
I watch myself watching myself thinking about writing something down.

Poetry after the Recent War

After an idea, a tactic, an ambiguous renunciation, of César Vallejo

For Sterling Plumpp

Blown to a tatter by wind, the cry of one gull or mew of one cat sounds nearly the same as a
        fleeing child's cry near dark.
Should I try to refine the paced unfolding of my syntax?

The appointed and the elected yawn after eating, they travel to games and medical examinations in
        bombers, but in public they condescend, shuddering with a repressed paroxysm of triumph.
Should I rework an unsatisfying rhythm?

The president of the nation lied about everything and hid his crimes and was elected and then
        withholding his plans from all but his most trusted parasites he rushed to war.
After that, devote a year to a poem in Chinese stanzas?

The excitement of the elected as death approaches swells and swells like pus in a boil; and the
        citizens wait and trust.
Should I control more carefully the scope of my allusions?

The generals calculate a future count of skulls.
Should I confer with my colleagues about the analysis of discourse?

Revolutionaries and revolutionary poets argue in a secret meeting about who is friend and who is
        enemy, and the enemies of those who are right to rebel must die.
Should I reconsider my punctuation?

In the recent war, before the soldiers were sent into combat, they were ordered to dig fifty
        thousand graves in the sand.
After news of that, should I elaborate a simile?

When the war was on, the fifty thousand graves proved to be an unnecessary scruple.
Thinking back about those buried in their trenches, should I change the narrative voice in my poems?

The war roared far away like a furnace whose white flame feeds on dark straw.
Should I count out syllables and stresses?

My countrymen were dropping bombs on people and on the place where writing was invented and
        where the first poem to be written down— a prayer to a now-dead goddess of harvest—
        was impressed on a surface of smooth damp clay.
Shall I consider whether I am more in the print or more in the oral tradition?

"This company is a lethal weapon," Capt. Larnell Exum, commander of Company A, said proudly
        as his men prepared to board their helicopter. "We're going to deal some death. And
        this is what we're fighting for," he added, whipping a pair of women's black silk
        underwear from inside his helmet.
Should I try to make less use of symbols?

The television fanfared with timpani and trumpets the solemn exciting entertainment of the deaths
        that had been scheduled for the evening news.
After that, should I spend a while searching for a rhyme?

To object to death brings accusals by righteous love-of-death and attacks by smiling love-of-death.
At such a moment, I should study the variations of the myths of Dionysos and Coyote and Staggerlee?

Compassionless brutalized sons are mobbing the excited streets to try to give birth to a giant
        father who will love and kill them.
Should I sincerely invoke a muse?

"This is the headquarters of my counterpart," the general said, and the press corps laughed, then
        the videotaped image of an apartment building in a bombsight turned to outflung dust
        and fell and disappeared.
Should I perfect the delicacy of poetic closure?

"Like shooting fish in a barrel," "like a turkey-shoot," "like a video arcade," "like roaches when
      you turn on the light," four pilots said to television reporters after climbing out of their
      planes.
Should I ponder the master tropes of metaphor and metonymy?

There are toy soldiers because soldiers are the toys of power.
Should I rank my words on my page like a phalanx of purified diction?

There are museums constructed like castles and mansions because art becomes mostly the trophy
      of wealth.
Therefore shall I recite my poems under bridges and in the catatonic corners of soup kitchens?

And anyway, a lynching is going by with a man on its shoulder.
Should I spend a half-hour on a problematical stanza?

Ancient lost goddesses of grace are weeping with grief far away in the place to which they were banished.
Shall I posit an aesthetic experience?

Mothers who taught their infant sons peekaboo two decades ago are crying with grief, thrown to
      the ground by news of irrevocable death.
Should I analyze the linguistic components of infant babble?

Fathers who smoothed the foreheads of fevered young daughters are shaking with grief as
      irreversible death shrieks in their ears.
Shall I outline the elements of poetry?

Men and women who lay limb to limb with women and men and men and women they loved are
      neither men nor women now with the inhuman moaning that grief pushes out of their
      mouths.
Shall I say to the rose, "Thou art sick"?

The many dead lie torn and akimbo like dolls silently weeping; those hurt but still living
    scream or faint or, looking at the television pictures of the dead lying torn and
    akimbo like dolls, watch and are silent.
Shall I frame in anthropological terms why the objections to war are so few and do not prevail?

The church on this side of the war holds sacred two crossed pieces of wood stained with
    blood—a simple instrument of torture that might as well be a spear or a gun.
Shall I compile all the meanings of the allegorical lily?

What used to be real is pale and what is unreal—like a sporting event or ice inside the skull or the
    crazed frenzy of climactic explosions—becomes all real.
Shall I invent a riddling rattle inside the dry belly of a poem?

                                23-26 February—September 1991. Wars.

Interview with an Upside-Down Old-Timer

I was lucky or far-seeing enough to understand
when I was younger that I could not learn
what I needed to learn
from poetry,
even though everyone else read poetry all the time,
it was almost all that they did.

I did poorly in school for this reason.

I was stubborn and did what I wanted to do:
felt a tremendous excitement over the athletes
and their games, even though scarcely anyone
else paid them any attention,
praised them even if I was the only one.
And was the only one, if I had to be,
to use all my money
to buy things, the only one to rush
through channels
for that sensation of speed, not moving
through places but moved past by the images.
I never felt, afterward, that I had wasted my time.
But it feels lonely to be different.

My father worked hard all his working life
and I believe I never was able to get out
from under his bad example.

Bad Families of the Western World

Earth gave birth to Heaven and then
she slept with him, and by him had
more children.
                    But then Heaven tried
to push them back inside her womb—
(Angry at what she'd let him do?)

Later, hidden Kronos leapt up
behind his father Heaven and cut
off Heaven's balls.
                    But some years after,
this Kronos stood near at the births
of his offspring and gobbled them
alive as they saw light.
                    But then
the strongest, Zeus, whose mother hid
him till he'd grown, was helped by her
and tumbled Kronos down in turn.

But all the rest were weak as pups.
Zeus ruled them every one.
He toyed with goddesses and girls.
He did not pity men.

Thus recorded in early texts,
the classic patterns, the spoiling rage,
the damaged lives now damaging—

thus fiends and furies, titans, giants,
much human life, so far; thus fathers
with their sons; and sons with theirs.

WEST

Oh *mater, mater,* I am sorry I spurned
at moments
your reasoning, your invention
of human rights
                    I am sorry that because I so hate
your slavery and weapons
your squandering sons (I too am one) and simpering daughters
(I know they're not your only children)
(I know not only you enslaved)
the police on your good side
                              police state on your bad
oh *mater*
        I spurned at moments your inquiries
your goddess of wisdom art and warfare
your god of wrath and sacrifice
your italics and saving contradictions

I am sorry
I threw off your beliefs
I mistook for your very awful own some
of what truly arises in all who have this forked body
                            these appetites
(whether near to you or beyond
your captains and factors)
(But who is beyond them now)

Weren't almost all your auguries wrong but still
I am sorry oh *mater* if I ever disparaged your movable type
I am sorry the tracts became uninhabitable

I am sorry, oh *mater*, you married
so many of your children to each other
in smoky hovels and on wind-scraped streets
shadowed by the winter edges
of such gray builded heights and billboards crackling
with unattainable color
(You permitted did you not my arguments
You invited resistance and revision
with the which to define yourself more strongly)
                    (defend yourself)

Oh *mater, mater,* I am sorry I keep quarreling with you
Sorry I said those things
                        I have said
so many things (as you taught me)

I am sorry I stopped my music lessons—
the piano frightened me sometimes
(It's so big and heavy)

I am sorry that so many of your children
at the twitch of their wants have
triggered their rage
                        against each other
Sorry that you too let them do it, gave them
the idea to do it
Sorry that it's against
                        each other that they do it
(Like your sisters you have an unpleasant liking
for sudden mayhem and ironic bloodshed and you
have given the best instruction of any
for the fabrication of explosions,
the organization of mechanized extermination)

(But yes, all right, don't…
Please I agree it was caesarean and minotaur sons,
not you, who
engineered, whose architects of suffering… giant mills…
chattels… executions for the infraction
of existing… I can't say it…
They were your sons, though)

(I am sorry)

I am sorry that I hated your hoarded collections
I am sorry that I so love them
It was yourself that you enriched with your raids it was
yourself that you trenched and looted so that
in this wing or in that wing you
could exhibit what you taught us to prefer of you
and of the others…
                              (Without those whom
your agents destroyed
but whom you said you were saving
How could you have been saved
How could you have even come into your glory
How could you)

(You did not give birth only to glory
I mean, to glory only
And not only you gave birth to glory)

You lied
You called your far-flung conquered, "savage"
but did not so name your nephews
whose garrottes and massacres, whose
ecstasy of letting blood you authorized
(I will try to be fair—as you taught me, also—and think
on universal infamy, as well)

I am sorry
            you revealed the golden mean to those
who built such temples
to money
such rational greed
on a scale of stony wealth that beggared
the rest of us
            our dwarfish
heavy depositing of mere coin

And then on wings of stealth and ire
Doth fly our wealth to further war
To plough the bloody ground with fire
To turn the garden to a scar

I.e. for then by electronic data transfer
if not with antiquated tangibleness in a courier's bag
our wealth flies
            (Why I must ask at
this point did you make us want
to comprehend)
            out on infinite loan
flung across sanctuaries and suburbs
to the commanders who set the dashboard controls
of remote damage and accelerate their sunglasses
I am sorry
Oh *mater*

There was an idea
an ideal

In my low pockets I keep the currency you paid me
Wages of polished teeth of dead captives
I did not want them captured

(I never said they should be attacked
I don't think I even knew it was happening
What was I supposed to do)

I renounced your first and last great poets, exhausted
and exalted by warfare
your captured obelisks
your hippodromes and encyclopedias
your architraves and eudaimonía
your gazetteers and your famous gaze

Oh *mater* I am sorry
I am sorry I spurned
your precepts and preceptorials
your insignia and violin
your magnetic resonance imaging
your theomorphic imagining
even the incarnation of your last god

I have been angry
There was a time when I loved you too much
Your cuisines and lexicons, your cadmium red, your medicine
You made me love you
You made me
I hate your mills the echelons the market-mind
the dowries and quitclaims and proceeds

And Father punishes and punishes
I have asked his forgiveness many times
I have begged
but he does not listen

Hurriedly he returns to his theaters
of conquest, of congress, of contest
to his camps oh now I have said it

his solutions provisional and final
(I know, I know, you cannot control him)
He returns to his favorite poem (*Iliad*)
He returns to his favorite novel (*Crusoe*)
his favorite markup and depreciation
his forms triplicate
his dials and domes
illusion and illiteracy
misericord and the membrum virile
and the images of nakedness
(which excite him)
(well why shouldn't they)
that you gave him

I am sorry
I am sorry I spurned
your
at times
how could I not
it was just because of
      my anger at your rationales
      my anger at your courts and balance sheets
      at the seven-year and thirty-year and hundred-year bullet-pocks
            in your stone façades
      your judges and generals and CEOs and shills
      my anger at tithes and mitering
      at classification by pistil and posture
      at the excited predation of calm bankers
            proposing a fall in the exchange
            and sawmilling a people
      at patriarchs and arches
      at great marble shrines and little wooden ones
            to an instrument of you know what
      at cosmetics on the pretty mannequins
      at the excarnation on your hillsides

of assassinated children of the uprising
at the speed of images transmitted as an eerie flickering
over the hard dry dusty ground on which
your audiences hunker at twilight
at the human caryatids holding up your massive systems

Yes I spurned your calculus and incunabula
your inoculations and precious alphabets
but also your missionaries and commissars
your colonies
your plutonium
it is all so

I would never give up your authors
your string quartets
and certainly not the man playing his violin alone, under a tree
and certainly not the woman singing
nor even the piano in its big rich room
For the sake of my tears, of my pity
Forms
My form
They help me feel the form and the pity
I would never betray

When we clay ones hold our offspring
toward the light of a little hope and we dwell
for the eternity of a few seconds in the laughter
of even one of them
This much we are given
oh *mater*

I stand beside our Father's cold casket
and wonder why his body is not here
and look over my shoulder at you
and then what do I feel

You are greater than
your children
say you are but they have
not admitted
how fully you come down
by way of all whom you have consumed
all whom you are... (I don't want to say it)

drawing from them your mind
that came to full thought
only because it encountered that
which by itself it had not thought
and those whom it had not known

I hate not knowing, it's my weakness, I got it from you

Wanting to be your best child
and your worst
I'll be your body and antibody
born into your hierarchies and luck
dying to change them
I know how to be grateful
I am trapped in my grateful hatred
of you
I love you
Of course I love you

THE HELL OF THE ENCHANTERS-FOR-HIRE

After a line of Bertolt Brecht

We left behind the slope of the disenchanted
and reached an alley at whose other end
a glittering city lay. "These are enchanters,"

my guide said, signalling to me the spent
figures who trudged along in the false light.
Their billboards blazed with what they'd never meant.

("'Twas such illusion that they sold and bought.")
Eyes sealed, ears stopped, an unrepentant chorus,
they croaked what we could hear but they could not:

"What is not, is; and what we say it is
is how it will appear—and what appears,
now is, and only is; we say it is."

Trying to see, to sense, unable to hear,
they blundered down the path toward alley's end
from which they came back quieter, streaming tears.

In agitated haste yet with practiced hand
they groped each other's pockets or a purse—
not to steal, but to stuff some money in.

Their mouths would make a sound, a kind of hiss,
that disinformed and lied and alibi'd
with lips that still could imitate a kiss.

They uttered pleas of innocence, they cried
precisely accurate mendacities
that echoed down the alley amplified.

Meanwhile the city lights—as if to please
even these blind—sizzled, roared, burst and bruised
the air with sparking wattage, a switched-on striptease.

Eager still to claim they were excused
for their hypocrisies as patriots,
the enchanters pled. My guide saw me confused;

"Their only cause," he said, "was corporate,
their hymn, a jingle praising liquid assets,
their faith, in power and military might.

"With proud, unholy loyalty—coquettes
to CEO's, dictators, pols and brass—
they held no ideal above their own deceits.

"Cawing plausible lies, they're official crooks
who preyed on fears they'd first created—a ruse
that gave them pleasure in itself, these flacks.

"All used words in order to bemuse,
wrote spin, PR, fake news. The chance to lie
was what not one of them could once refuse."

I noticed now that with every word and sigh
these sinners spoke, they drooled vile excrement,
which they wiped away with paper currency;

this, on another, as I'd seen, they'd spend—
a rank forced gift. The fecal taste, they spewed
and spat, in vain, as if it might relent.

"Most vile, they always claimed the Godly good
of man their goal, while at their raging whims
so many died or lived in servitude.

"They thought the victims of their snares, whether numbed
by goods or dumb with pain, entirely blessed.
And anyone who wouldn't buy, they blamed.

"They called their terror freedom, blackmail trust,
death life, lies truth, filth cleanliness, the salt
of blood a sweetness.... They excused the worst."

Then, struck anew by the force of this insult,
my guide cried out, "Such criminal rhetoric!"
Afraid that he himself might swoon, I knelt

beside him, took his hand, and loosed his cloak.
Recovering, he said, "Within such skulls,
what is there?" Studying them, again he spoke:

"Meanwhile, inside the limousines and malls
of politics, appointees raved against
the truth, for power's sake. They put on sale

"to privilege and hatred the arguments
that raised and sustained them in their frequent polls.
They prevaricated and prayed in self-defense.

"Some unwitting Academic kin, loud gulls
who convinced themselves, if no one else, they stood
against the sordid demagogues and pols,

"counter-raved, in a gleeful wrecking mood,
declared all utterance invalid, and swept
from words the meaning that anyway they'd hated.

"(But those are found on a lower slope in a crypt
where not one torment suffered has a name,
so according to their lights does not exist.)"

Before us moved the enchanters, foul and lame,
a ceaseless train. My guide looked up, then bowed
his head, though whether in despair or some

great-souled pity, I did not know. My dread
grew suddenly, I thought I might pass out
in the smoke and ozone, but he rose and led

me on till I regained my near-dead spirit.
I hesitated—my own tongue begrimed
with soot and meanness, but he called for wit,
and took me toward an even darker crime.

Reminiscence of a Distant Exile, Or, Song of Houston

Some people see the autumn colors and feel sad.
The place I'm from, a summer sadness is what it has.

The half-developed no-man's land I used to walk
in a new Sears suit, from the Cotton Exchange to the bank,

carrying deposits, my first summer after high school,
I hear that you cross now in an air-conditioned tunnel.

At Main and Texas, most were resting in the colonnade
of the Rice Hotel, some were just trudging sadly ahead.

Tall cooled glass huge centers of commerce and supply
that no one has to leave for anything till the still-hot end of the day

can assuage discomfort or a rash, but can't lessen the sadness
of heavy cologne, mowed grass, an evening tank of gas,

or of the freeway at 2 a.m. when the window air coming in
is hot and your pressed clothes have turned to wet swaddling.

Air-condition all the apartments, malls and cars,
cool offices until we freeze in summer sweaters—

but there's nothing anyone can do to appease or change
deserted humid yards at a hundred degrees, the mangy

lots, the exposed hot white sidewalks, the buzzing hedges
avoided by all forms of life a little large,

such as the tired students who, crossing from class to dorm
in the heat, lose the thought they'd only recently formed

in a room cold as ice, completely sealed from the blast,
from happy scratching grackles and from engine exhaust.

Oh sad is the early morning already at 85,
sad the coffee that's no hotter than the car outside,

sad the late hours in the bar or ice-cream parlor
that's the last haven of the day from sweaty clamor,

sad oh sad remains the cook-out by the lake,
the mad-dog patient man waiting on the pier for a strike,

sad the trip home to the heat-loving water roaches,
sad the rotting swings on uninhabitable porches,

and sad the bills for electricity and beer,
sad the sleepless nights in stifling heat or artificial arctic air—

May to October heat, hot vacancies, hot rain,
weeds running a fever, headaches inside headaches—

but you've got to gather the courage to live until November,
you've got to go out now and get into that car.

Figure of Speech

In the New World anthropological museum I saw at some distance a standing terra-cotta figure and walked to it, and found first the surprise of survival of so large a piece of brittle clay. The museum has very little information in it; there was none about the figure of the man, a priest perhaps, who was wearing what I fancied might be a coat or costume of feathers, and with eyes shut and mouth formed like a tenor's holding a high note, he could have been chanting or singing.

At a dinner I asked a local anthropologist about what I'd seen, and he told me the figure was evidently that of a man flayed alive by priests who had believed that to insure the return of spring one of them or more must wear another man's skin in a ceremony of invocation. What I had taken for feathers or leaves all over the man's body was instead the sculptor's stylized representation of the tissue and fat under his skin, exposed by the flaying. And his expression was not of singing or even speaking with the intensity of anger but simply of a killing pain; a scream.

When I was a child, I heard someone say, "I'm going to skin you alive."

SUMMER NIGHT

The moment toppled over as soon as I woke into it.
The cry of a small person in a nightmare was still fading.

I got up into the heavy bedraggling heat and saw
in the next doorway, between her bedroom and the pink hall,

Mother waiting for an answer to her question.
In the hallway hung the cloud of images from her troubled sleep.

Her nightmare was in a cemetery and we stood in it still.
All around her lay the desecrated monuments

of her own feelings, defaced and overturned—
Who could have done this?

Beyond her, creeping with fright from tomb to tomb
while clasping the box of ashes of yet another feeling,

which she would soon bury, was herself, also.
And hiding from her behind the headstones, ready to return,

was the gang of vandals, each of them her, too.
She took my hand, hers as light as a sparrow,

the look on her face, in her eyes, the question,
all the questions, I have not answered.

Historic Site

Fathers, my father among them, began to build—after they scraped and fenced their acres and trucks brought piles of raw yellow lumber. (Among and under the boards nested scorpions and snakes.)

The river I lived on was only a ditch, the ruins I roamed lay invisible in the footpaths through treeless fields where at most only hunters or later a wagon or certainly a surveyor might have passed. (A cannonball pitted by rust, found, how we envied him, by another boy, was the only evidence that anything human had ever happened where we lived.) And my ocean was the emptiness of the horizon.

Over and through our new realm flew female wasps drooping in the air as they hovered down on the hunt. I watched them also build mud chambers up under new shed-eaves and then come from afar flying with heavy numbed prey they dragged and pushed inside where for a moment they too stayed; then came crawling out.

In a book my mother brought me I read that on each pulsing sleeper entombed alive a wasp left one egg that would hatch and eat. A wasp would seal each of her chambers shut. And in a season each would be unsealed from inside by a new wasp that crawled out into the daylight whole.

Among torn webs, the emptied rows of hard mud cells would still be clinging to the wood under the eaves in cold weather.

A child reading books, imagining ruins and a river and someone alone under the sky after rain in the fields, was alone under the sky.

(Mother—I thank you for bringing me that book.)

When the ditch filled to the rushing top after storms I was kept away from it.

For a while after we dwellers settled those fields I believe there remained, by some kind of faint implication, a trace of early human passage. You felt it when you stood alone in the heat of the day too far from the house to be seen by anyone.

All that place filled up, and the only ruins there are the memory and trace of the unruined emptiness that was.

Or the old pronunciation of a word or a name now spoken differently, or the path now under pavement that used to lead out to a shed (under the eaves the female mud-daubers toiled and reproduced themselves) and then beyond the shed into openness.

It was perhaps one hundred years after my childhood when I came from my father's grave to the vanishing buildings of my home and I surveyed this acre of the half-fallen light of his bewildered years and I shook with cries of the kind that do not come out into the air until their wings are formed.

MESSAGE TO BE PUT INSIDE A BOTTLE

Out of the time that was our deaf present
we both spoke and were spoken

With embellishment and intricacies
of pleasure and sorrow
we sought to add to our remembrance

·

When we lived we were
straw in the fire of states

In the mind of the daytime sky we were only clouds

Water in the mouth of deserts

We were a song in the unlistening ear of the night

And infants were poems of hope spoken by their mothers' bodies

·

We became words on the tongues of our own households

We were the botched drafts written
by an alien history
in the power of power

We tried to revise ourselves—
each of us a stanza of five rhymes
Each one of us half-rhyming with every other one

And our lives were the etymologies of our deaths

SHORES

But for the loud ocean it is quiet

Bright clear long still day of summer

Under an unappeasable meridian

Air pungent with sun-heat and wild herbs crushed underfoot

or jasmine or woodsmoke coffee gasoline

The sandy rocky ground hot the air warm

Out in the broad dark bay only a few pale fishing boats

A taverna nearby with only shading reed mats for walls and roof

One man drinking inside one man outside pounding an octopus

The waves push shimmering planes of light up the flat beach

Inland, not far, is a city on a millenial hill

            •

A wind a storm will turn this light
to a clouded moiling wracking of the sand
when wide seething waves topple forward falling heavily
beating and beating the shore
slowly unendingly as if for a reason

·

For good auspices we sacrifice a bull or twenty beautiful great bulls
or if we have
only a lamb then only a lamb
to God
We sacrifice it to God we ourselves go without it we sacrifice it for God

·

The men who massed on this shore put on helmets covering crown and nape and countenance

Such helmets are masks they frighten they threaten

The mask hides the warrior's face

The masks hides what is on the warrior's face

from his victims from his comrades

·

Not that God needs the bull or can use it or even exists in that way
but that our sacrificing it makes us think about how we should exist

·

This army our own

Our colors our insignia our partiality

Its spears its tanks its craving on this hot day for ice ours

Protecting us destroying everything everyone that would harm us
everyone that would not harm us
disincarnating them all

Transporting
our glad souls out of us
to a cloud of no one of us but of an all

that does not know any one of us

Above the moving army the exulting cloud
that absorbs us lifts us into itself

The army its excitement and dread steadily contained advancing
into the world it seeks

the world it seeks to uncreate

It seeks to uncreate that city

city on the millenial hill

The churning cloud of dust and spirit
over the soldiers is gray and white and red
like waves of weirdly-lit storm-ocean

Cries

Oh God our God look back over your shoulder at this

Metaphor

They make a jumbled mountain of ships
of the dead and hurt, stacked in the weighty sunlight,
sailing nowhere, and the wind blows past them.

Change of Heart

In the ring-lit arena of an empty parking lot late at night, resting there, in your car, away from other things and everyone, you I understand all right: you with your hyponymy and favorite pens, your collar stays and starred paragraphs, your weariness and dread, your wounds and sores of spirit, your desk and your debt, your schedules and disappointments, your seatbelt and shopping list, your gait and posture, your sudden moods of despair.

Do you really think a complaint would help? Would getting out, within view of the watching lake, taking a spot under a streetlight and reciting a few pleas to the neighborhood make a difference?

How about picketing one of the radioactive embassies instead? How about arriving with no luggage for a long stay in the daylight? How about abandoning all plans of order and control and flying home on your own wings, any way you feel like going? How about lightening your tread across the town's aching shoulder blades?

How about a raid to stay the slaughterhouse hammer? How about a leaflet in favor of revolutionary conscientiousness? How about getting on with it, this ordinary life? How about asking someone for directions? How about bringing up a laugh out of that chest of yours where pirated happiness lies uselessly locked, gleaming for no one in the dark? The lake is watching. Your watch is ticking. Spend the doubloons! Throw them to anyone who asks! What did you ever think you were saving them for?

2

Homage to Longshot O'Leary

For Thomas McGrath, 1916-1990

1.

October 1, 1989. The recent history was told to me before I arrived—back and forth between hospital and nursing home Tom has been carried. He rises and falls like a tide of stubborn unwillingness to leave this life. In his true mind—which, I am told, still flashes out of him once in a while with the old fiery impatience and wit— he is certainly angry that he has no strength left to end his own suffering. Before this decline, he told me on the telephone that he didn't want something to happen that would put him at the mercy of pain and helplessness, he had decided to kill himself, but at the pleading of his son, he did not.

Now he is forced to live what he had hoped to avoid.

Early for my ride to the hospital, I step into the little grocery store where Tom used to shop. I see all the everyday foods and humble ordinaries out of Tom's reach now. But I think I dwell on it more than he would: even when he has had a lot to complain of, and has complained, there has been something resolute and forward-looking about him. Even when things have looked bleak, he has pressed on. He has persevered without being necessarily optimistic or cheerful. Yet even when not very cheerful, he has had a ready laugh and ready hope. I heard that Tom said to K, "I think you're a sad man who has had a happy life, and I'm a happy man who has had a sad life."

I leave the grocery, and here outside the door is a precious artifact: a wooden produce crate stamped *California Kiwi*, into which the store people have dumped some dubious fruit and vegetables—for free? for the homeless? The crate speaks of agriculture, labor and the pleasures of exotic sensation. And it's attractive in itself— the clean wood, the colorful label. Taught by Tom to appreciate this but not to idealize, I then think: What of those working conditions and wages? Perhaps this unsold food won't be wasted.

In Minneapolis the civic tone is charitable, the atmosphere tolerant and encouraging of good efforts. Over the door of another store I saw a sign reading "Please Leave All Bags, Briefcases and Large Stringed Instruments at the Counter." There should always be such relics as stringed instruments and steam-engine threshers, and celebrations like Tom's poems to remind us of human hands at work and play.

Back I wander along the bland wide avenue to Milwaukee St., where Tom led me on a slow short walk when I last came to Minneapolis—that was before he fell, injured his head, grew weak and unsteady from the damage, could not eat properly and never has, since. Everything is bare and exposed a little too nakedly, a little too openly, in a Midwestern way under the unforgiving breadth of the Midwestern sky. The small houses face each other across a walkway and esplanade; no cars; flower beds planted with humble marigolds. Poems are one of the ways we speak ourselves to life—our own poems and those of others, like Tom's that are full of his love of the colorations of words, the rhythms of American English, his engagement with his causes. Tom's view: idiom is the mother of poetry; history the father; marigolds the banners. "Pipsissewa and sassafras," as his poem has it: little plants offering a blossom or a root, bearing the names given to them by the music of speech.

2.

Men and women and girls and boys labor in
granaries, glass factories, hospitals,
in plenary assembly lines and at no-vote sewing machines,
in republican ditches and judiciary fields,
in pain under transmissions and over fires,
deafened around airplanes and between flagmen,
weary on streets and in subway stops,
through bad weather and foul spillage,
behind desks and at the beck of telephones,
among chemicals and gangsters—

not made more worthy by this labor
nor less, but if they could would simply own
their used and unacknowledged worthiness,
would own if only they could
their own time of living the unreturning hours

even if elsetimes they may be entertained by
the transmutations of TV and gladiatorial shopping
and are thus educated
to what they are given to know and
something more—a knowledge in the labor like
the salt taste in sweat or tears

3.

T and I were in Minneapolis in January of 1987, three days asking Tom questions,
taping everything. T was probing Longshot's politics and personal history, mostly;
he was working on the essay which would not be published till after his own
sudden death, that so shook Tom and grieved me, only a few months after this
moment. And I was asking about the poems. I wanting secrets; T wanting an-
swers—T who had brought nightmares with him from childhood, then found their
echo and new visitations in his years of reading and thinking about the German
death camps, his mind strained by the scale of defeat even as he found in it the
seeds of survival and dignity; seeds planted in winter... Thinking of the myths of
annihilation that exhilarated the murderers, I also think of a counter-image—our
Mayflower, our myths of privileged origins. More than four million persons are
said to be present-day descendants of those Pilgrim emigrants! In the death camps
that T wrote about, genealogical time ran backwards; the camps consumed not
only the six million persons in them but also their potential progeny, the offspring
that were not to be born to the millions who were killed—of whom how many
would there now have been, parents, children, grandchildren, great-grandchil-
dren? The camps were for destroying the origins of the unborn.

Tom went to the *Book of the Hopi* for adequate symbols in *Letter to an Imaginary Friend*—symbols from that region of indigenous cultures and (by 1610, well before the Mayflower arrived with its self-mythologizing passengers) alien governors from Spain. Poems like Tom's—rich in lingo and lived history—seem to me like lessons in a spiritual genealogy that we have to construct for ourselves, that will tell us, if we want to know, from whom we are descended in spirit, whom we are free to claim as our protecting fathers and mothers to help us against the owners and inquisitors, sadists and thugs, beastly and heroic conquerors, and against the merely indifferent, through whose gauntlet we must so often be running as we try to reach the sowing and the harvest, the building and the making, the feast, the carnival, the romance, and peace.

And I came to choose the Tom in the poems as one of these fathers—to be taught by the movement of breath in his lines, the peculiar surprising and some-time visionary metaphors, the forms that he said he liked "to rotate a little," the permissions granted by his boisterous vocabulary, the world hefted in the working hand, and the working hand surrounded by wildflowers and shipyards, the long shots, the lost locomotives, the last clattering of the horses' shod hooves, the call to respond...

4.

Complications and responsibilities of the appropriate
response in these days when cold gazes measure
the range of projectiles, the grievance,
the building site of another fenced camp,
when no single store or catalog offers better value,
when spectacles of thrilling outrage
swing back and forth before all eyes
and injury comes in solids, stripes and checks

·

A car is always on fire to one side of the highway,
a woman walks up her steep unpaved hill, the weight of the morning
marketing in her string bag, and passes a man
coming down through the mud, talking on his cellular phone
as he carries an empty plastic bucket to the one well

•

At the steps of a closed church
on a street I think might be Avenida Salsipuede
a blear-eyed starving dog stands motionless
very slowly turning its head to watch us
in the hot sunlight as we walk past,
offering us its own thought
in its own language
which for this once
we can easily comprehend

•

I would like to be as simple as a starling in the rain
Sometimes I would like to eat only seeds, like a sparrow

•

But the work one might do

5.

A wave rises
            coming in at
                        an angle to the beach

Another wave falling back is cutting
                              under
the coming wave
                    The coming wave
rises bulging upward
balances on its own moving thickness
begins to curl forward at the top
                              starts to topple
roars along churning
                    sand and foam as it slides
reaches up
            the wide wet shallow smooth slope of sand
faster and farther as it
                         thins to a sheet
and then gives out
                    touches the last grains
(but not quite the line
                of dry wrack left
                              by high storm-tides)
And it slides back
                accelerating and gathering itself
slices
        under the next wave

Speed without haste
Contest but no malice

We hurry to live
while the waves come in and come in
while up and down the hospital hall
the nurses amble to answer the patient

6

Our New World ruins
           Empty factories, scorched
shops and businesses in the districts
of the leveraged takeovers and the riots
Our blazing-up balloon-frame fires
Our kinds of monuments of our kind of tragedy and romance
(of working hours, bus-seats, poll taxes…)

Even Sears closes, on this street and that
Some of a forest disappears, birds dislodged
(a literal forest here
           a figurative one there
with first-growth health benefits
           and a company meadow)

These could be old stones—of an abbey, a fortress—
but it's just an American retailer's wall
Sometimes the pressure of feeling,
like a firehose, like a steam cooker, who knows how long
a man, a woman, a father or mother, can contain it…
It's going to explode, it may come
from elsewhere, *that* argument, *that* unhappiness,
that impossible desire, that heartbreak
for the baby of the family, but wherever
it came from, now it is flowing out at
a stone in a wall, this wall along the gritty street

We wanted to get the little guy something

Chicago—no illusions here of fortresses or abbeys or ancient walls
Only our old brick of industry
           our teetering pinewood 3-flats

No romance of any glitter
of the money that was churned to make more money

This wall was just the money that didn't make more money
This was just a raising of edifice and ornament and sales floor
out of labor and grain, mills and railroads,
sewing machines, metal stamping, plastic molding, retailing

Meanwhile an argument, a human dissonance,
pain and harm, accusations and denials as this
little family come some miles to the big store
turns back from the locked doors toward the el stop

Nor do the empty floors pay anyone's wages now

7.

Tom was perhaps not so preoccupied with instances of suffering as with systems of exploitation. It's I who am stricken by the plights and episodes; Tom was more concerned to oppose political and social structures. I am touched by scenes and stories, and Tom too was angered and bitterly amused by anecdotes and tales and cautionary inspiring examples, but I think the moments that spoke to him had to be representative rather than dramatic. He was more political and I am more emotional. He could be saddened but I am sad. He was always looking past the instance for the pattern. He believed in his cause and I weigh beliefs. But aren't my categories too crude? Did he not suffer at the news of suffering? I haven't got this right, exactly. The Wall came down in eighty-nine, and Tom came down soon after, leaving this only physical world, down from the ruined ideals murderous and stony in that wall, and already he was past being able to think such things through any more, so we didn't get to talk about it. "Of course," he said one time, "those are deformed societies."

8.

As was taught, we are
                    only sparrows but

sparrows that take
                    a little longer to mate

sparrows that read
                    little sparrow books

sparrows that tell
                    sparrow stories

sparrows that invent weapons

sparrows that take power

other sparrows that resist

watch

remember

and others...

9.

Walking through Our metonymous Town I think I hear Longshot
giving an unguided tour,
pointing with that black-gloved hand of his to

Rightfully-Ours Inflated Realty
Sentimental Mass-Speak Greeting Cards Co.
Gov't-Protected and Bailed-Out High-Dollar-Welfare Mobile-Capital Bank & Brokerage
Most Dangerous Working Conditions Mfg.
Dispiriting Wage Service Co.
State-Sponsored Xenophobia Consultants, Ltd.
Nasty, Brutish & Short, Attorneys at Law
Students Working Against Poetry (SWAP)
Global Murdering, Inc.
Fear & Reassurance Local Evening News
Happy Kitchen World Advertising
Muscled-Man/Pouty-Woman Plumbing
Chicago Society for Professional Secrecy
AAA Orphanage Supply Co.

10.

But in addition to venting his potent dispraises, Tom could also celebrate and commend. Simple things pleased him into writing his praises, as they did Neruda, sometimes. I knew Tom only for the last few years of his life, when he lived in that apartment on 22nd Ave. South with only a few furnishings, a hundred books, and this that and the other, when Jesus Christ those long cigarettes he smoked lighting one off the other, that macabre black glove that couldn't keep his left hand warm (the botched operation at the VA hospital), a kind of ski glove so puffy that it seemed not to contain a hand at all when he wore it, it was an inflated thing at the end of his arm, his dictionaries his gravelly laughter his smoker's cough, his story of the box of papers including manuscripts of *Letter to an Imaginary Friend* taken by mistake by the garbage men from the curb in front of his house on moving day, the phone beside him now on the vinyl couch (he says into it, laughing ruefully, "I'm in deep shit here, trying to explain what is going on in *Letter!*") and when Martin comes in one day bringing Tom groceries Tom introducing him by saying, "This is the McGrath that should have been the poet, he's the great one for stories and songs," and Martin, looking like a younger and stronger Tom, grinning and ducking his head. And the several worlds seen by Tom (several worlds even unto the Fifth World of the Hopi) existed mostly without knowing Tom was in them; and poetry, in which Tom built new windows and then threw them open, exists mostly without other poets even knowing Tom was writing. Oh poets like me of egoistical hesitations—world and poetry were rising and brewing with his secret yeast. His unabashed pleasure in saying—whether the thing said was compacted of metaphoric intensities or as common as the rain.

11.

"It's gonna be cold
"colder than a witch's tit
"colder than a barrel of penguin shit
"colder than the hair on a polar bear's ass
"colder than the heart of the ruling class"

and he laughs, shaking his head

12.

Nevertheless, on the greenswards of the park in the democratic summer air
we gather for an internal combustion picnic
                                        before the fireworks
begin
        on the Fourth

                        We call up our rattling, groaning histories
our fled time

We mark
the anniversaries
               of our families
in the several great realms of the New World

We say again the phrases and tales we have best remembered
The young mothers so close that they nursed each other's babies
in the old neighborhood
                              Sunday dinners in the old kitchen
The lawsuit
Those bills for Dad's illness
Sister's great performance but then she gave it up

Our causes and klatches
The good works on this street or that
Good persons

Old World always becoming New
                         New World also…

Our five-act dramas
               Our Chevrolet births and Ford divorces

We hear a kind of poem
                         in the noise of the highway and the ocean waves
in the sound of the shouts and a backfire or a gun
                                   within the whispering
of the wind in the leaves—a poem
                         about the same rain falling
on tin roofs and penthouse terraces
                         on small-farm crops and country clubs

About our flying first jobs and our Tylenol retirements
the pennons and etymons of gladness and despair
the little pieces of the-story-of-it-all

that are our own—stories even saddening ones
that remind us of the paths down which
we've come hurrying or hesitating
                              Hustling

Advancing, fleeing
Wandering...

Our chosen mothers and fathers, if we can find them, helping us along...
Or not...

Some people knocked down by life
                              Others knocked open

13.

Oh Longshot! Surely some revelation is at hand
(your black-gloved hand)
somewhere in
this first or third or only world of ours, a shape
       that should have been a flying tiger
       a universal free election of the Buddha-nature
       a crowd of generals and CEOs levitating in a mountain temple, renouncing their desires
       a media magnate weeping over the Sermon on the Mount
       the satori of Karl Marx and/or Adam Smith
is scanned as selling power, and even now
is morphing towards L.A. and Hong Kong

14.

(Interviewing him:)

             Straw and apples
                      the farmyard
the bindle stiffs
          Anger and hope and love
Comrades
        Labor and weariness and delight

His cantrip circle

          His elaborate joke of the hornacle mine
The cold military boredom in the Aleutians
while elsewhere his brother was killed in the war

                          Reznikoff's
lanterns around a manhole and Dr. Williams's luminous empty
room in Nantucket...
          "Objects exist in a fluid world"

The League of Happy Teamsters
              The shape-up
The organizing

Proud of his expulsions from the Party for not writing
in a way the workers could readily understand
but proud too of his own loyalty...
On the one hand Cock-eye Dunn and on the other Stephen Duck
("the thresher poet")

          Small triumphs and holding his ground
but mistakes, too... ("Oh, I snaffled it," he said, hanging his head)

And: "Logic
is the money of the mind"—not to disparage reason,
as it's our only tool against the irrational, but wrong reason:
when it's not the partner of festival,
                    of carnival, feeling, love…

Hart Crane
          Lorca
                    Cisco Houston
                              Brecht

Rukeyser   Fearing   Roethke   MacDiarmid   Krishnamurti

"My experience," said Longshot, "has been an eccentric spiral…"
and with the index finger of his good hand he traced it in the air

Coughing, shifting in pain, sitting hunched
under a blanket that covered his shoulders…
                              "I hate paper"—
holding up that black-gloved hand:
                              — "especially after *this*."

The Murmansk run
                    The Lolo Trail

                              Enlightenment

The lifelong weavings of his engagement
Poems both tactical (aimed at rousing people to act,
aimed at *moving* them—
                    Longshot, his face
tilting, a wreck, offering the example
of a buffalo dance before the hunt)
                              and strategic

(aiming to "expand consciousness")

and the great desideratum:

the "flying tiger" of a poem that is both

15.

His anger wasn't pessimistic or defeated—his nature
was to celebrate: "There are so many things I want to praise
that I don't know where to start."

One place he started was in
the lips and eyes, thighs and hips, of women whom he loved
in the heaven of a hayloft

or an open field,

in L.A. or on an island in Greece...

Whether calling them by name or not,
in the remembered time of his *Letter* he placed them,
set them—although in the poem and it seems in his life
their apotheosis was of the body only, not the mind...

Except for the firebreathers?—Emma Goldman or la Pasionaria
or Flynn: "the rebel girl," her stone marker says, near
the graves of the Haymarket martyrs in Chicago...

And having entered a bodily heaven with women,
Longshot went ahead alone, leaving them behind,
making his own representative way toward
the charmed and humbly holy circle he revered

of those who (men
and women) with their hands and backs

persisting even when work

means seven days a week
$$\text{build and dig, sow and harvest,}$$
herd and assemble, cook and sew and clean and assemble…

So he set the women
$$\text{(mother;}$$
and the women he desired)
$$\text{in the great poem like jewels}$$
(Not what they wanted or deserved…)

(He said he was talking with his first publisher, Alan Swallow—decades ago—and
Swallow said, "Do you know where your books sell the best?" And Tom said he
said, "No, I don't. They don't seem to be selling *at all*." And Swallow said, "There's
a whorehouse in Wyoming where they sell more of your books than anywhere
else. The madam is crazy about your books, and she makes all the girls read them,
and they turn the johns onto them.")

16.

A man's gonna sweet talk and give you big eye, my momma done told me (Ella singing it)
In a coffee house I have a little extra time
The register ratchets and stutters, a confluence of ancient and modern,
     tokens of wealth toted up by electrons
The random, even speckling of the wallpaper does not represent the clumping of matter
     or of meaning
It must be we seek meaning because it has some survival-value
Our appetite for a meaning fullness

The young woman who serves me coffee is cheerful
I steal time—but only from myself can I steal it, it can't be stolen from anyone else
Could I steal some of the tiger's time? Could I give it away? Could I give it to Tom?
Last night I dreamt a hummingbird alighted on my hand, tiny, exquisite, blue

But it turned out to be a kind of intensely vibrating slug that could leap to my hand
        from the same vine-flowers at which hummingbirds were sipping
A slug the same extraordinary color as the birds, even shaped like them, with a little pointed
        appendage that was a false beak
And a dollar-sign mark on its back
(I shuddered and shook it from my hand)
What is the value of the meanings I perceive?
One of High-Plains Schoolmaster Tom's Elementary History Lessons:
                Values are always changing…

Symbols shift their allegiance…
(The women in his mind symbols)
(Tigers are often symbols)
(Burning bright, or flying)
(But what are the hummingbirds and the slugs?)

Now I must go outside, down the street,
up into the antiseptic room,
and see him as—he said and said
when he was still filled with saying—
he never wanted to be seen
                        As he wanted never to be

After I finish drinking this coffee and pay for it

May I have more, please?

She is so cheerful

17.

October 2, 1989. Saw Tom again in the hospital. He wasn't as alert as yesterday,
tho' he did recognize me, and also recognized B, who had brought me to the
hospital this time. Tom is too weak ever to stand again. He can smile but he cannot

convey what he is smiling about; he cannot laugh any more. He can move his right arm to rub his left; yesterday he could wiggle his foot, today he doesn't. He would yawn like a small monkey. Horrible reduction of the great attentiveness, mildness of the strong spirit, silence of the golden tongue.

Yeats wrote in his journal, "The soul is an exile and without will," but the soul of Tom, not exiled in his lines but alive there in its proper home, and with will aplenty, was, even then, at that moment of Tom's leaving, and is now, shaking its striped head, glaring with fiery eyes, lashing its tail, and beats its wings once, twice, testing its strength, ready.

18.

In a later year

beside the broken sidewalk

    in the representative and democratic sunlight

a heteroglossia of silken hues

    in the crocus and narcissus tolling

a wild mixture of tiny peals and pleas

or it might be

    in this beginning of spring

this end of winter

    pipsissewa and sassafras…

• • •

Photograph by Miriam Berkley

REGINALD GIBBONS was born in Houston, Texas, and attended public schools there. *Homage to Longshot O'Leary* is his sixth book of poems. He has also published a novel, *Sweetbitter* (Penguin, 1996) and has translated Spanish and Mexican poets, as well as Euripides' *Bakkhai* (to be published by Oxford University Press). From 1981 to 1998 he was the editor of *TriQuarterly* magazine. Now a professor of English at Northwestern University, he also teaches in the MFA Program for Writers at Warren Wilson College.